AMAZING
MAMMALS

AMAZING
MAMMALS

Sandy Creek
NEW YORK

An Imprint of Sterling Publishing
387 Park Avenue South
New York, NY 10016

Editorial and design by
Amber Books Ltd
74–77 White Lion Street
London N1 9PF
United Kingdom

Contributing Authors: David Alderton, Susan Barraclough, Per Christiansen, Kieron Connolly,
Paula Hammond, Tom Jackson, Claudia Martin, Carl Mehling, Veronica Ross, Sarah Uttridge
Consulting Editor: Per Christiansen
Series Editor: Sarah Uttridge
Editorial Assistant: Kieron Connolly
Designer: Keren Harragan
Picture Research: Terry Forshaw

ISBN 978-1-4351-4276-3

For information about custom editions, special sales, and premium and corporate purchases, please contact
Sterling Special Sales at 800-805-5489 or specialsales@sterlingpublishing.com.

Manufactured in China

Lot #:
2 4 6 8 10 9 7 5 3 1
09/12

Contents

Introduction

Mammals are warm-blooded (which means they can make their own body heat even when it is cold outside), they have fur or hair, and give birth to their young rather than laying eggs. Mammals include some of the most fascinating creatures on the planet; they live on land, in trees, at sea, in the air, and under the ground.

American Bison

American bison are the largest land mammals in North America. Bison bulls have huge forequarters and big heads. This very strong and solid body is used in battles for superiority during the breeding season. The leaner hindquarters help give speed when running.

Buffalo Herds

▶ Massive herds of American bison, also called buffalo in North America, used to thunder across the plains.

WHERE DO THEY LIVE?

Once found across North America's prairies and high plains, now confined to a few reserves.

North America

Offspring

◀ Dramatic breeding battles between the bulls ensure that weaker males are not allowed to reproduce. Bison were almost wiped out by hunters in the nineteenth century.

FACTS

SIZE

- Diet consists of grasses and other plants.

- Lifespan is up to 25 years in captivity and 15 years in the wild.

- The largest North American mammal.

DID YOU KNOW?

◖◗ Both sexes have horns. They are wider, longer, and less curved in bulls.

◖◗ The shoulder hump is a thick pad of body tissues covering bony growths from the spine.

◖◗ The thick mat of hair on its head is used to sweep away deep snow and uncover vegetation. It also protects the skull.

Woolly Coat

▶ A woolly "cape" covers the head, neck, and forelegs. The dark, shaggy winter coat falls off in spring. It is replaced by a light, short summer coat. Coats are usually brown or dark brown. White ones are very rare and are seen as sacred by native North Americans.

Bactrian Camel

The domestication of these camels began more than 4,500 years ago. Today, there are more than two million of the domestic variety, but the wild population is endangered. They live in harsh environments where they are exposed to extremes of temperature throughout the year.

WHERE DO THEY LIVE?

They are found in Asia's Gobi Desert and have been introduced to the wild in Australia.

Gobi Desert

Australia

Coat Change

▶ The Bactrian camel's dense winter coat may fall off in huge chunks as the weather changes.

Facial Features

◀ Long eyelashes keep sand out of the camel's eyes. A long beard runs down the underside of the throat, with some hairs as long as 10 in (25 cm).

FACTS

SIZE

● Camels graze on grass and taller plants.

● The humps are a fat store, indicating the camel's condition.

● The lifespan of a camel is up to 40 years.

DID YOU KNOW?

Both toes on each foot spread out as the camel walks, stopping it sinking into sand.

Camels are valued for carrying heavy goods in packs slung over their bodies. They can also provide milk.

You can tell a well-fed camel because it has upright humps that do not slope to the side.

Ships of the Desert

▶ Camels have been described as "ships of the desert" partly because of their rolling gait. This comes from their unusual way of walking. Both legs on one side of the body move forward together, followed by the legs on the other side.

Dromedary Camel

All camels store fat in their hump. They use this fat as a food supply when they have little to eat in the desert. Their fur keeps them warm during the cold desert nights and protects them from the hot days. The Dromedary camel is also known as the one-humped camel or Arabian camel.

Hump

▶ The dromedary has two humps. The second one between the shoulders cannot be seen clearly.

WHERE DO THEY LIVE?

Northern African deserts and across Central Asia to Mongolia. Also introduced in Australia.

Asia

North Africa

Australia

DID YOU KNOW?

🌢 Only the large hump in the middle of the dromedary's back can be seen clearly.

🌢 Camels can be bad-tempered and will spit, bite, kick, and even vomit half-chewed food at each other.

🌢 The dromedary can lose almost half its body weight but not be in permanent danger.

Camel Racing

► Camel racing is a popular sport in desert countries. These animals are well-adapted to desert life. They can survive for a long time without drinking, as they get some of their fluid from eating plants. When they do drink, dromedaries can swallow up to 66 gallons (250 liters) of water at one time.

Calves

◄ Dromedary calves can walk by the end of their first day. They stay with their mothers for one to two years, until they are old enough to look after themselves.

FACTS

SIZE

• Typical color in the wild is light brown.

• Hard skin forms on the camel's knees where it lies down.

• The nostrils can be closed to keep out sand.

Four-horned Antelope

The four-horned antelope is usually found close to water, near streams and rivers. They like to be alone and are fast runners. This way they can protect themselves. They are not easy to spot, although they are active during the day.

WHERE DO THEY LIVE?

Hilly and highly mountainous areas throughout India and Nepal.

Nepal

India

Strong Legs

▶ The antelope has long, strong hindlegs. They help the antelope leap and run away from predators.

Hunting

◀ The antelope's four horns stand out, but this makes them popular targets for hunters. Only around 10,000 four-horned antelopes survive in the wild.

FACTS

SIZE

- They live for up to ten years.

- They are herbivores, eating only grass, herbs, and fruit.

- They can make a husky call if threatened.

DID YOU KNOW?

- The second pair of horns grows when the antelope is about 14 months old.

- A gland in front of each eye makes a scented liquid. The antelope uses this to mark its territory.

- Because more and more forests are being cut down, there are fewer places for the antelope to live in.

The Horns of the Antelope

▶ The horns are smooth and conical in shape. The rear pair grow up to 4 in (10 cm) long and the front pair reach about 1.5 in (4 cm). The female antelope does not grow horns. She has a smaller and more delicate head than the male.

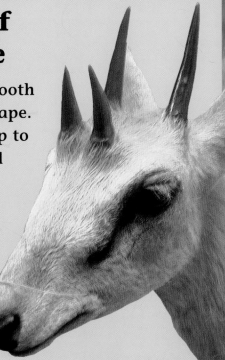

Giraffe

The giraffe's extraordinary height is a great advantage both for feeding and defending itself. Their body shape means that their heart must work twice as hard as a typical mammal to pump blood right up to the brain. The giraffe's heart therefore needs to be very large; it can weigh up to 22 lb (10 kg).

WHERE DO THEY LIVE?

They live in South, East and central Africa. Prefers open woodlands and grasslands.

Africa

Giraffe Herds

▶ Giraffes move in loose herds, walking (sometimes running) across the African savannah (grassland).

DID YOU KNOW?

 The horns are bald in male giraffes.

Giraffes can see over greater distances than any other land animal. This helps them to spot predators from a long way off.

Giraffes stand up for most of the time, because lying down makes them easier to attack.

FACTS

SIZE

- Lifespan of around 20–25 years.

- Diet of shoots, leaves, and grasses.

- The tallest of all living land animals.

Reaching High

► The giraffe's tongue can be 20 in (50 cm) long and is dark blue or purplish. With the upper lip, the tongue pulls off buds and leaves from trees. Like most mammals, the giraffe's neck has seven vertebrae (bony parts). However, the giraffe's vertebrae are very long.

Lengthy Limbs

◄ Up to 6 ft 6 in (2 m) long, the legs are very powerful and are used to lash out in defense. For a giraffe, lowering the neck to take a drink can be a difficult task.

Moose

This species is known as the elk in Europe and the moose in North America, where the elk is a completely different type of deer. Moose are herbivores (they don't eat meat). A moose can eat up to 44 lb (20 kg) of vegetation a day. They will sometimes graze on water plants. Moose live alone and do not form herds.

Water Lovers

▶ Moose are excellent swimmers. They will sometimes wade out into water to eat water plants.

WHERE DO THEY LIVE?

Northern woodlands around the world from Alaska and Canada to Siberia.

Canada   Siberia

Young

◀ Adult moose have brown fur, but newborns have reddish-colored fur. Young moose stay with their mothers for almost a year, until the next calf is born.

FACTS

SIZE

● They eat grass, shoots, leaves, and aquatic plants.

● Hollow hairs in the coat help insulate the moose from the cold.

● They live for up to 20 years.

DID YOU KNOW?

● Antlers can tell us two things: how old the moose is and where it comes from.

● The upper jaw and lip droop over the lower jaw. This helps the moose tear leaves from thorny twigs.

● Moose are solitary, spending most of the year alone.

Moose

▶ The male has antlers until the end of the mating period, which is around October. A new pair starts to grow during the spring, reaching their full size between three and five months later.

Pygmy Hippo

The pygmy hippo may look like a smaller hippopotamus, but it has many differences. Its back slopes forward, to help it push through the thick rainforest. It spends less time in deep water than the hippopotamus does and so it has smaller nostrils.

The Senses

▶ Its eyes, ears, and nostrils are all high on its head so that it can see, hear, and breathe while almost underwater.

WHERE DO THEY LIVE?

Africa

In West Africa, mainly in Liberia, but also in Guinea, Sierra Leone, and the Ivory Coast.

Feeding

◀ In the wild, the young do not leave the water to look for food with their mother. Instead, they stay and hide in the water until the mother returns.

FACTS

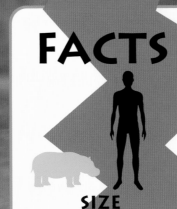

SIZE

- It lives mainly on land.

- It eats a variety of ferns, shrubs, and fallen fruit.

- It lives up to 35 years.

DID YOU KNOW?

🐾 The pygmy hippo lives alone, in pairs, or beside rivers and swamps in dense rainforest.

🐾 The pygmy hippo lies in muddy water or hides by riverbanks during the day. It comes out at night to feed on the forest floor.

🐾 It spends less time in the water than the larger hippopotamus.

Pygmy Hippo's Skin

▶ The pygmy hippo has smooth, dark skin. It would lose water rapidly in dry air, but it stays moist in the humid (wet) conditions it lives in. The feet are broad and have four widely spaced toes to help support the hippo on soft ground.

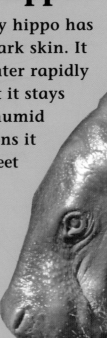

Reindeer

The reindeer, also called caribou in North America, is a common animal of North America and Eurasia. It is very well adapted to life in the cold, far north. It has a thick coat that keeps the reindeer warm by trapping air. Also, this trapped air makes the reindeer float a little bit, helping it to swim better.

Herd Animals

▶ Reindeer move in herds. They travel huge distances with the changing seasons.

DID YOU KNOW?

- During winter, it can slow down the speed at which it digests food to make it last longer.

- The hooves are broad to make it easier walking on snow and mud. Also, the hooves are cup-shaped, making them ideal digging tools.

- Reindeer can cover 600 mi (1,000 km) looking for food.

WHERE DO THEY LIVE?

In the far north of North America and Eurasia.

North America　　**Asia**

Eyesight

◀ Reindeer are the only mammals that can see ultraviolet light. This helps them see objects in the Arctic that blend into the snowy landscape in normally visible light.

FACTS

• Reindeer nostrils warm up the cold air before it enters the reindeer's body.

SIZE

• Their hooves are like a sponge in summer. In the winter they are hard and dig into the ice.

Antlers

▶ The reindeer is most commonly recognized by its large branched antlers. It's the only species of deer where males and females have antlers. The bull's (male's) antlers can grow up to 4 ft (1.2 m) wide. The males use their antlers in battles with other males over finding a mate. They are also used for defense.

Wild Boar

The male boar is built for fighting. It is armed with slashing tusks and has tough, thick skin to help it during battles with rivals. It is a strong fighter and will protect itself fearlessly. Wild boars are sometimes called pests because they dig up the ground for roots and this kills plants.

Galloping

▶ The boar usually trots along, but it can gallop quickly over short distances.

DID YOU KNOW?

0 The boar walks on its enlarged third and fourth toes, which form a cloven (split) hoof.

0 The snout moves in a circular motion when the boar is foraging (looking for food). The nostrils close to stop dirt from getting into the snout.

0 The legs are short, but have powerful muscles.

WHERE DO THEY LIVE?

Native across Northern and Central Europe, the Mediterranean, and much of Asia.

Europe

Asia

Piglet

◄ The piglet is born with a striped coat. This makes it harder to be seen among the trees by other animals that might attack it. The stripes disappear after six months, when the boar is stronger.

FACTS

SIZE

● Wild boar live for 15–20 years.

● The domestic pig is the same species as the wild boar.

● They eat vegetable and animal material.

Teeth and Tusks

► Two enlarged canine teeth in the lower jaw form the tusks that stick out of the boar's mouth. The curved upper canines fit behind the tusks. The male's tusks are much larger than the female's. They are used as digging tools and as weapons.

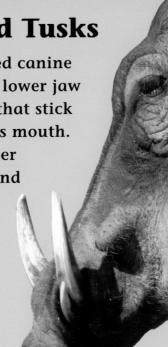

Wildebeest

Once a year, thousands of wildebeest gather into herds. When it is the calving season, they make round trips of up to 1,000 mi (1,600 km). This is known as migration. The wildebeest move to reach better pastures so they can eat well. They also need to find water supplies, and to escape from other animals that might attack them.

WHERE DO THEY LIVE?

East and southern Africa.

Africa

Vultures

▶ Vultures follow wildebeest migrations because they feed on dead wildebeest bodies.

DID YOU KNOW?

 Wildebeest is Dutch for "wild cattle."

Their main predators are lions and hyenas, who will mainly attack young wildebeest.

The wildebeest has a muzzle on its mouth like a lawnmower. This makes it easier to eat short grass.

FACTS

- They are very strong and can injure a lion.

- They can run at 40 mph (64 km/h).

- If in danger, they form a group with zebras in open savannah.

SIZE

Wildebeest

▶ Wildebeest calves are born in the middle of the herd so the other herd members can protect them. They can stand and run only a few minutes after they have been born. The females in a herd will give birth within a few days of each other, which swamps the area with calves, making it difficult for predators. This is known as the "dilution effect."

River Hazards

◀ Wildebeest face many dangers when they cross rivers. Many of them will be eaten by crocodiles and hundreds are lost during the migration journeys.

African Lion

The lion is very strong. It is at the top of the food chain in the savannah where it lives. It can hunt alone or as part of a group. Lions hunt very well on their own, but they are better at catching large prey when they work together.

WHERE DO THEY LIVE?

Sahara Desert

Africa

In Africa, south of the Sahara Desert. A small population also lives in India's Gir Forest.

Shaggy Mane

▶ The male's mane helps him look threatening. It might also protect his head and neck during fights.

Canine Teeth

◄ Long canine teeth can cut into a victim's neck or spine. Carnassial (cutting) teeth cut through flesh. The tough tongue helps to shear flesh from the bones.

FACTS

SIZE

- Lions live for up to 16 years.
- Only male lions have a mane.
- Female lions are the pride's (group's) main hunters.

DID YOU KNOW?

 Young lions do not help to hunt until they are about 18 months old.

 The claws grasp prey. To keep them sharp, the lion pulls them back into sheaths (pockets) that protect them.

 Their very powerful legs are good for sprinting and attacking large prey.

Lion Pride

► Lions live in a family group called a pride. This is usually made up of 4–20 females with their cubs and two or three males. Everyone has their job in the pride. The lionesses hunt, and the males stay behind to defend the territory and protect the young.

Cheetah

The cheetah is the fastest land mammal on Earth. Its body is adapted for high-speed hunting. It can compete with the many other predators of the savannah. The cheetah's long and powerful limbs allow it to accelerate very quickly. It has a flexible spine that arches and springs back like a bow, allowing it to make giant strides.

Sprinting

▶ The cheetah can sprint at speeds of up to 75 mph (120 km/h) over short distances when chasing prey.

DID YOU KNOW?

 The claws never pull back fully: they stay partially extended for extra grip.

 The long tail helps to balance the cheetah's body as it twists and turns at extremely high speeds.

 The large eyes point forward so they can spot where their prey is very clearly.

WHERE DO THEY LIVE?

Africa

Found in southern and eastern Africa, but rare in northern Africa. It survives in Asia.

FACTS

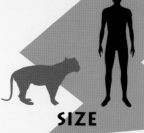

SIZE

- A cheetah can cover almost 33 ft (10 m) in a single stride.

- It can accelerate from standing to top speed in three seconds.

- Fastest land mammal.

Camouflage

▶ The coat provides camouflage for this daytime hunter. It makes it hard to see in the tall savannah grass. Every cheetah has a unique pattern on its coat. The spots can be up to 2 in (5 cm) in diameter. The color can vary from tan to buff. The underside of the belly is white.

Cubs

◀ Females live alone except when raising cubs. The mother leaves her cubs at 18 months. Males stay together, but females leave the group at two years old.

Coyote

Coyotes are found in deserts, grasslands, mountains, and city suburbs. They are expert hunters that use their sharp senses to find a wide variety of prey. They can travel in large groups, but generally hunt in pairs. There are usually six coyotes in a pack, including a pair of adults along with young coyotes.

Hunting

▶ The quick and clever coyote uses its keen senses to find and follow its prey over long distances.

WHERE DO THEY LIVE?

Throughout North America, from Alaska east to Nova Scotia and south to Panama.

North America

Pups

◀ The young emerge from the den three weeks after birth. Male pups leave the den for good after six years. Female pups remain with their parents to form the new pack.

FACTS

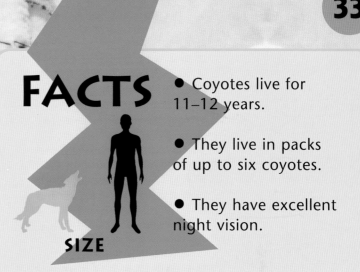

SIZE

- Coyotes live for 11–12 years.

- They live in packs of up to six coyotes.

- They have excellent night vision.

DID YOU KNOW?

 Coyotes' hearing is very sharp. They also use their ears to communicate their position of authority and their mood.

 Coyotes from desert areas have reddish coats. Coyotes that live in woodland areas are more of a gray color.

 They are most active at night time.

Coyote Howl

▶ The coyote holds its head up, with jaws wide open and canine teeth exposed when it makes its distinctive howl. The howl is a series of high-pitched yelps followed by a long wail. Howls are most often heard at dusk or during the night. Howls call the pack to the pack leader and are most common during the spring and fall.

Eurasian Otter

The otter is well-equipped for life in the water as well as on land, so it enjoys the best of both worlds. It is a powerful swimmer and a very efficient aquatic predator. It has a streamlined body that makes it quick and agile when hunting in the water.

Nostrils

▶ The otter's nostrils are high on its nose. This lets it breathe while most of its body is underwater.

WHERE DO THEY LIVE?

Across Europe up into Scandinavia, North Africa, Central and Southeast Asia.

Europe

Asia

North Africa

Whiskers

◀ The Eurasian otter has long, sensitive whiskers. These pick up underwater vibrations that help the otter find its way and track down prey.

FACTS

SIZE

- They live up to 20 years in the wild and 9–10 years in captivity.

- The tail is more than half as long as the body.

- The nostrils close when the otter dives.

DID YOU KNOW?

- An otter keeps its outer layer of fur waterproof by grooming it several times a day.

- It leaves scented droppings to tell other otters its sex, age, and readiness to mate.

- Its long, sharp canines are used to grab fish. Its carnassial teeth are used to slice through bone and fish.

The Otter's Fur

▶ The otter has two types of fur. An outer layer of thick guard hairs is coated with oil to make it waterproof. An under layer of short dense fur keeps the otter warm in cold water. The coat is generally dark brown on the back and paler underneath. Otters have webbed feet that help thrust them forward when they swim. The large hindfeet have more webbing. These provide most of the power when the otter swims.

European Badger

The European badger is an expert tunneler. It has a strong body and powerful claws to help with digging. It will also fight back if it is cornered by an enemy. Badgers dig underground burrows called setts. These have many tunnels and chambers.

WHERE DO THEY LIVE?

Britain and Ireland eastward across much of Europe, including Scandinavia and Asia.

Europe

Asia

By Night

▶ European badgers come above ground to look for food when it starts getting dark.

Cubs

◄ The top female badgers sometimes kill the cubs of less powerful badgers. There are one to five badgers in a litter. The badgers are born pink.

FACTS

SIZE

- They live from 3–15 years in the wild and 19 years in captivity.

- They live in groups called clans.

- Badgers have short and stocky legs.

DID YOU KNOW?

 Badgers spend days on end underground in the winter.

 The large skull has massive jaw muscles. These give the badger a powerful bite. The teeth are adapted for eating a wide variety of food.

 Badgers are social and live in groups of around a dozen.

Black and White Stripes

► Badgers have black and white stripes on their heads. These go along the sides of the face to the neck. Their coat is thicker in winter than in summer. A coarse, grizzled coat of longer hair lies on top of finer, thick underfur.

Giant Panda

The giant panda is a species of bear. Although most bear species eat meat, the panda has a special vegetarian diet of bamboo grass. The problem is that once a bamboo grass has flowered, it dies. This means many pandas risk not finding enough bamboo to eat and so might starve to death.

WHERE DO THEY LIVE?

Found in the Sichuan, Shaanxi, and Gansu provinces in China.

China

Bamboo

▶ Pandas spend most of their waking hours eating bamboo leaves and stems, which is quite a poor diet.

Saving Energy

◀ Pandas live in cool, damp mountain areas. They have developed thick fur and a bulky body to help them save energy.

FACTS

SIZE

● Newborn giant pandas may spend nearly seven hours a day suckling at first.

● Pandas spray urine to mark territory. They do this whilst doing a hand stand against a tree so they can spray high up.

DID YOU KNOW?

🐾 A newborn cub is 1/900th the weight of its mother.

🐾 The eyes have vertical slit pupils like those of a cat. The Chinese call it *xiongmao*. This means "giant cat bear."

🐾 They have a wrist bone like a claw on each front paw. This works like a thumb to aid grasping.

Body and Coat

▶ The giant panda has the same sort of body shape as all bears. It has short legs with flat feet. It has a body shaped like a barrel, and a huge skull with long jaws. It has a springy, oily coat that protects it from cold and damp. The colors give excellent camouflage.

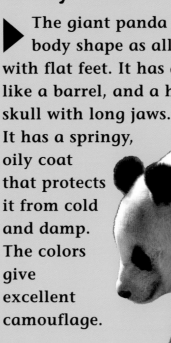

Grizzly Bear

The grizzly bear has a bulky body that helps it survive some of the coldest winters in the world. It is very strong but is also surprisingly quick over short distances. It can attack large or fast prey. It can hunt a variety of prey but prefers to eat roots and berries.

Fishing

▶ Grizzly bears will wade into water to try to catch salmon.

WHERE DO THEY LIVE?

In North America, mainly in Alaska and Canada. There are a few in the USA.

North America

DID YOU KNOW?

 Grizzlies that live in the far north are usually larger than those in the south.

 The shaggy, brown hair helps keep out the winter cold. The grayish tips give the bear a "grizzled" look.

 Scratch marks made on a tree may mean there is a bear in the area.

Cubs

◀ A female usually gives birth to two cubs per litter. She cares for them for up to two years. She will not mate again for another four years.

FACTS

SIZE

● Grizzly bears are mainly vegetarian.

● They can run at speeds up to 25–28 mph (40–45 km/h).

● They can climb and swim.

Important Tools

▶ Like other bears, the grizzly does not have carnassial (shearing) teeth to slice into flesh. Instead it has broad molars to grind up plant material. Grizzly bears have a moist nose and wide nostrils on the snout. These provide their most important tool: a very sharp sense of smell.

Spotted Hyena

The spotted hyena, unlike the striped hyena, mainly hunts in packs. It kills live animals rather than eating already dead meat. It kills zebras, cattle, sheep, and goats. It hunts mainly at night and sleeps during the day. It lives in groups of up to 80 hyenas. These groups are called clans.

Young

▶ A female carries her baby in her mouth. Young spotted hyenas are called cubs, pups, or whelps.

WHERE DO THEY LIVE?

Sub-Saharan African countries such as Tanzania, Zimbabwe, Ethiopia, and Kenya.

Sahara Desert

Africa

Hunting

◀ Hyenas can hunt alone, in small groups of two to five, or in large groups. They chase their prey, often running as fast as 31 mph (50 km/h).

FACTS

SIZE

● Females are larger than males and dominate them.

● They can digest skin and bone.

● After 10 days, cubs can run very quickly.

DID YOU KNOW?

 The spotted hyena is also known as the laughing hyena. It is related to cats and not dogs as is often thought.

 It has a large heart, forming 1% of its body weight. A lion's heart is only 0.5% of its total body weight.

 Its bite is 40% stronger than a leopard's.

Hyena Cubs

▶ On average two cubs are born in each pregnancy. Cubs are born with soft brownish-black hair. Unlike other meat-eating mammals, hyenas are born with their eyes open. Cubs often attack each other shortly after birth. A quarter of cubs are killed by brothers and sisters in their first month. After two months, cubs start to develop spots on their coat.

Meerkat

Meerkats live in warrens. These warrens have more than one entrance, which helps the meerkats to escape back underground if danger threatens. The members of the group each take turn to be on guard. They keep lookout for about an hour while the rest look for food. They watch out for predators such as birds of prey and snakes.

Standing Tall

▶ The meerkat stands up tall like this when it is on the lookout for predators.

WHERE DO THEY LIVE?

Southern Africa, from Angola and Namibia into Botswana and South Africa.

Southern Africa

Domed Skull

◀ The skull is like a dome, with a pointed muzzle and small ears at the sides of the head. The eyes are large and high in the skull, so meerkats have good eyesight.

FACTS

SIZE

● Meerkats are very friendly with other meerkats. They work together as a team.

● The long, slim body helps it slip quickly underground when danger threatens.

DID YOU KNOW?

🐾 Up to 30 meerkats might live together in a warren.

🐾 The tail is used like a third leg. It helps to balance the meerkat while it stands up for long periods.

🐾 Each front paw has four very long, strong claws that are used for digging.

Eyesight

▶ The meerkat has sharp eyesight with good color vision. It can stare hard into a bright sky and spot birds of prey from far away. It has oval pupils that are horizontal. This helps the meerkat get a wide view of its surroundings. It has a pale, sand-colored coat that gives good camouflage against the soil in dry regions.

Polar Bear

The polar bear has thick fur that helps to keep it warm so it can sleep through biting blizzards or plunge into the Arctic's near-freezing waters. Its large size and round shape help protect it against losing too much heat. A 4 in (10 cm) layer of fat lies under the skin, which is black to absorb heat.

WHERE DO THEY LIVE?

Northern coasts of North America, northern Russia east to Siberia, Greenland and other Arctic islands.

Greenland

Russia

North America

Seal Hunting

▶ Polar bears can scent an air hole in the ice made by a seal from over a mile (1.6 km) away. They wait for the seal to surface.

Cubs

◀ In the fall, a pregnant polar bear will dig a den in the snow. She will live here without eating for up to eight months. On average, she will give birth to two cubs.

FACTS

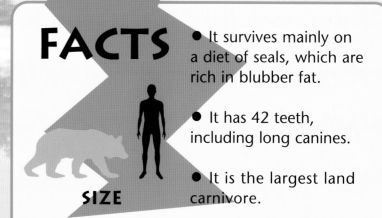

SIZE

● It survives mainly on a diet of seals, which are rich in blubber fat.

● It has 42 teeth, including long canines.

● It is the largest land carnivore.

DID YOU KNOW?

 The hind legs are used for steering and are longer than the front legs.

 The hairy feet act like snowshoes. They help the bear walk on snow and ice without suffering from frostbite.

 The bear's creamy-white coat blends into the landscape. It is also water-repellent.

Sense of Smell

▶ The polar bear's head is long and tapering, with small ears and powerful jaws. The bear's sense of smell is very good. However, its eyesight is not especially good for a carnivore. The nose is highly sensitive. A bear can smell a seal carcass up to 20 mi (32 km) away.

Siberian Tiger

This is the largest of the nine subspecies of tiger. It is also the biggest member of the cat family. It weighs nearly 70 times as much as a domestic cat but is able to pounce more than three times its own length to catch prey.

Dense Fur

▶ The fur is very thick. There are around 7,500 hairs per square inch over the whole body.

WHERE DO THEY LIVE?

Now confined mainly to the Amur-Ussuri region of eastern Russia.

Russia

Amur-Ussuri ●

Offspring

◀ When born, the Siberian tiger cub is blind, has no teeth, and is no larger than a normal house cat. Female cubs stay with their mothers longer than males.

FACTS

SIZE

- Soft pads on the feet allow the tiger to walk silently as it hunts prey.

- It often travels hundreds of miles over harsh terrain in search of food.

DID YOU KNOW?

🐾 These tigers develop a big mane of longer fur around the neck in winter.

🐾 The stripes on the face and body are different in each tiger, making it easier to tell one from the other.

🐾 Tigers lap up water with their tongues like a domestic cat.

Ferocious Jaws

▶ The large skull gives a solid anchor for huge jaw muscles. The canine teeth are up to 3.5 in (9 cm) long. They are used to stab prey, while the carnassial teeth are used to slice through muscles and tendons.

Spotted Skunk

The skunk defends itself by spraying out a foul-smelling liquid. The spotted skunk's coloring is more complex than the striped skunk. The coat has both black and white stripes and other markings, with a white spot on the forehead.

Coat Color

▶ The skunk has a black and white colored coat that warns other animals not to attack it.

WHERE DO THEY LIVE?

North/Central America, including British Columbia, the USA, Mexico, and Costa Rica.

North America

Central America

Scent Glands

◄ A skunk sprays its scent by squeezing glands in its bottom. The stinking spray that shoots out should put off any attackers.

FACTS

SIZE

- They are excellent climbers and will nest in trees and attics.

- They eat vegetation, insects, and small mammals.

- They live for up to ten years.

DID YOU KNOW?

🐾 It hides in a den during the day, and comes out at night to hunt under the cover of darkness.

🐾 The tail is fluffed up and straight when it is under threat or trying to impress a mate.

🐾 Skunks are related to weasels, badgers, and otters.

Eyes and Teeth

▶ The spotted skunk has forward-facing eyes that give it good binocular vision. Binocular vision helps an animal to judge distances. This is a feature that most carnivores have because they need to spot prey. The spotted skunk has larger carnassial teeth than other skunks. These teeth are used to slice through flesh.

Gray Wolf

The gray wolf has long legs, large paws, and long-lasting energy. It can cover distances of 18.6 mi (30 km) or more at a 3.7–6.2 mph (6–10 km/h) trot. It was once one of the most widely distributed mammals in the northern hemisphere. Now hunting and the spread of cities have made its habitat smaller.

WHERE DO THEY LIVE?

North America   Europe   Asia

Remote areas of Canada, Michigan and Wisconsin in the USA, Russia, and a few areas of Europe.

Howling

▶ Wolves can communicate over long distances by howling. They also growl, bark, and whine.

Wolf Pack

◀ Wolves live in a pack that has a complex social order. The pack is led by an adult male and female. Usually only this dominant pair of the pack breed.

FACTS

SIZE

• Wolf packs hunt large animals such as caribou and moose.

• A wolf's hearing is 20 times sharper than a human's. A wolf can hear the howls of others up to 10 mi (16 km) away.

DID YOU KNOW?

 The gray wolf's coat color contains many different colors.

 The wolf's coat is made up of long hairs that are water-resistant. There is also a woolly underfur that helps keep it warm.

 Some gray wolves can be jet black, especially ones in Canada and northern USA.

Wolf Features

▶ The gray wolf's strongest sense is smell. The area around its nose is 14 times larger than that of a human. Its sense of smell is a hundred times more powerful than a human's. The powerful jaws are twice as strong as the jaws of a German Shepherd dog. Wolves usually stay with their pack for up to two years.

Vampire Bat

The vampire bat has broad wings that make flying easy. It has long, curvy, sharp claws on its feet and thumbs that help it climb over the warm-blooded body it is feeding on without waking it up. It uses its teeth to tear off a tiny piece of skin. Then it drinks the flowing blood.

WHERE DO THEY LIVE?

Central and South America, Mexico, Uruguay, central Chile, and Argentina.

South America

DID YOU KNOW?

- Vampire bats leave the group at nightfall to search for a sleeping animal to feed on.

- They spend the day roosting with other vampire bats, with which they form close friendship bonds.

- The maximum length of a vampire bat is 3.75 in (9.5 cm).

Coloring

▶ The body is a dark gray-brown above. The underparts are paler with brown-tinged fur.

Hearing

▶ Bats are the only mammals that can fly. They use sound like a radar. They send out a sound and then work out where they are from how long it takes the sound to echo. There is a sensor on the vampire bat's nose. This tells the bat where the blood of the animal it is feeding on is closest to the surface.

Wings

◀ The long, fine bones that support the thin wings are the bat's fingers. The wings are rolled up when the bat is resting or walking.

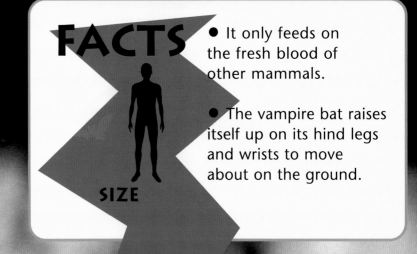

FACTS

SIZE

● It only feeds on the fresh blood of other mammals.

● The vampire bat raises itself up on its hind legs and wrists to move about on the ground.

Nine-banded Armadillo

These armadillos live alone. They make many dens, digging out the soil with their powerful claws. Unlike most mammals, armadillos have little body hair to keep them warm. This partly explains why they are such keen burrowers—they need to avoid extreme temperatures.

WHERE DO THEY LIVE?

Central America, and South America.

USA

South America

Nine Bands

▶ The nine bands extend around the center of the body, with shields across the rump and shoulders.

Armor

◀ The protective armor of the nine-banded armadillo is made of tough, bony plates covered by thick, leathery skin.

FACTS

SIZE

● They use their claws for digging rather than defending themselves.

● They mainly eat insects.

● They can live up to 15 years.

DID YOU KNOW?

🐾 The nine-banded armadillo can move surprisingly fast.

🐾 The nine-banded armadillo tries to outrun predators. Other types of armadillo roll into a ball to protect themselves.

🐾 There are nearly always four in a litter. The offspring in a litter are identical.

Sense of Smell and Taste

▶ The long snout has a sensitive nose and a long, sticky tongue. The snout is used to search through the soil and debris looking for insects and larvae to eat. Armadillos have a very good sense of smell.

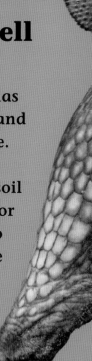

Western Gray Kangaroo

One of the largest kangaroos of Australia, the western gray feeds at night mainly on grasses. They live in groups of up to 15 called mobs. Males fight each other by boxing.

Cooling Down

▶ Kangaroos are not able to sweat, instead they lick their forearms, and the saliva that evaporates cools the animal down.

WHERE DO THEY LIVE?

They are found across the southern part of Australia.

South Australia

Enemies

◀ The Western gray kangaroo has few natural enemies. It is hunted by dingos, Australian wild dogs. Farmers are allowed to kill some because they eat farm crops.

FACTS

SIZE

● Males are up to twice the size of females.

● The western gray is also known as the red-faced kangaroo.

● It stands about 4 ft 3 in (1.3 m) tall.

DID YOU KNOW?

↳ Males are called boomers or stinkers because of their curry-like smell.

↳ When the males box, they lock arms and try to push each other over. They do this to show who is the strongest to lead the mob.

↳ Females are known as does or fliers.

Mothers and Joeys

▶ Pregnancies last 30–31 days. The mother gives birth to one baby, known as a joey. The joey then lives in the mother's pouch on her stomach for 130–150 days. In the pouch it can feed on her teat. The mother communicates with the joey using clicking sounds.

Koala

Although it is often described as a bear, the koala is actually more like a wombat. Both are marsupials, which means they carry their young in pouches. The koala eats the leaves of the eucalyptus tree. These are poisonous to most other animals. It eats during the night, but sleeps in the trees between 18 and 22 hours a day.

Offspring

▶ After leaving the pouch, a young koala will be carried on its mother's back.

WHERE DO THEY LIVE?

In Australia, from Queensland in the north through New South Wales to Victoria.

Australia

Sensitive Nose

◀ The large nose contains sensitive hairs. These allow the koala to tell the difference between many different types of eucalyptus leaves by their smell.

FACTS

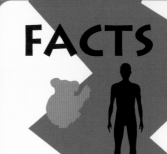

SIZE

● Koala young are known as "joeys."

● At birth koalas are no bigger than a small coin.

● They are fully grown by their fourth year.

DID YOU KNOW?

🐾 The koala has a special system in its stomach for digesting all the eucalyptus leaves it eats.

🐾 On its front feet the koala has thumbs, like a human's, which give it a strong grip.

🐾 Koalas have fingerprints just like humans do. Skin patterns help get a better grip when climbing.

Groups

▶ Koalas live in groups. Each koala in the group has its own area called a home range. This usually crosses over a little with the ranges of other koalas. Males often live alone.

Red-necked Wallaby

The red-necked wallaby's hind limbs (back legs) are very powerful. Tendons are tissue that connect muscles with bones. Inside each hindlimb of a wallaby, the tendons stretch. They act like a spring, catapulting the wallaby back into the air when it lands after each bounding stride.

Sensitive Ears

▶ The wallaby has very good hearing. As soon as it hears a predator approaching, it bounds away.

WHERE DO THEY LIVE?

Mainly in eastern and southeastern Australia.

Australia

Offspring

◀ The young will stay in the mother's pouch for about 280 days. Then the female and her offspring will stay together for a month, before separating.

FACTS

SIZE

- They feed around dusk and dawn.

- The red-necked wallaby is one of the most common species.

- They live up to 15 years.

DID YOU KNOW?

ᕹ The red-necked wallaby is shy and spends the day resting where it is safe.

ᕹ The long tail acts like the rudder of a ship. This helps the wallaby change direction when it is jumping.

ᕹ The tail also acts as a "third leg" to support the animal.

Fur

▶ This wallaby gets its name from the thick, reddish fur that covers its neck and shoulders. They have a black nose, black paws, and a white stripe on their upper lip. The fur keeps the wallaby warm in the cooler parts of its range. In the past, the red-necked wallaby was hunted for its fur and by farmers because the wallabies grazed on the farmers' land.

Sugar Glider

The sugar glider has a squirrel-like body and a long tail. They live in mixed groups of up to seven adults plus young, with territories. The territory is marked out using saliva and scent that comes from glands on their chest, pouch, flanks, feet, and at the base of the tail.

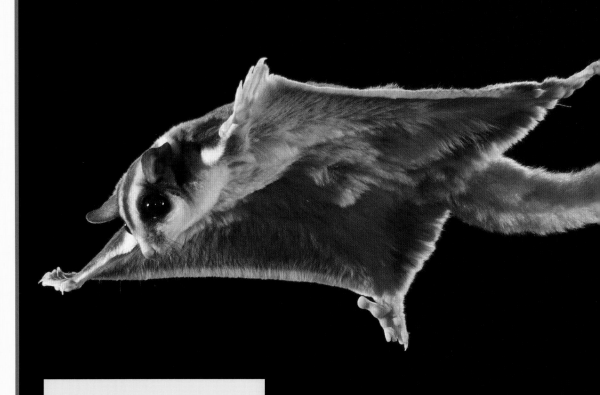

Gliding

▶ Thin skin (known as patagium) connecting its legs allows the sugar glider to travel from tree to tree.

WHERE DO THEY LIVE?

Australia (including Tasmania), New Guinea, and parts of Indonesia.

Indonesia

Australia

Feeding

◀ The sugar glider uses its sharp teeth to dig out holes in trees to reach the sugary sap. It uses its tongue to take nectar from blossoms.

FACTS

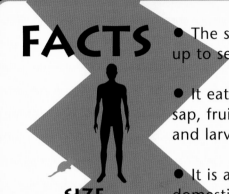

SIZE

- The sugar glider lives up to seven years.

- It eats nectar, pollen, sap, fruit, gum, insects, and larvae.

- It is a popular domestic pet.

DID YOU KNOW?

🐾 Small but long-clawed feet give the sugar glider excellent grip when climbing.

🐾 The sugar glider steers by pulling or loosening each patagium—the thin furry membrane between its legs. It acts like a parachute.

🐾 The sugar glider can fly up to 148 ft (45 m).

Useful Tail

▶ The furry tail helps the sugar glider balance when flying and climbing. It can hold branches and carry material for nests.

European Hedgehog

European hedgehogs come out at night. They are most likely to be seen on summer evenings after rainfall, when they come looking for insects to eat. As the fall approaches, they start to put on weight for hibernation, when they will hide away sleeping until spring.

Defending

▶ The hedgehog raises its spines in self-defense. The spines are also used like a cushion when it falls.

WHERE DO THEY LIVE?

Most of Europe and western parts of Asia.

Europe

Asia

Breeding

◀ Up to five young are born to a mother with each pregnancy. The babies' spines appear within a few hours of being born.

FACTS

SIZE

- They live for up to seven years.
- They don't have very good eyesight, but they do have a strong sense of smell and hearing.
- They eat insects.

DID YOU KNOW?

🖐 The hedgehog's sharp spines are about 1 in (2.5 cm) long.

🖐 The long snout has a sensitive nose, which is always moist to help its sense of smell.

🖐 In cooler regions, the European hedgehog hibernates during the winter when food is hard to find.

Prickly Spines

▶ There are approximately 5,000–7,000 spines covering the hedgehog's back. Each spine can move so that it can lie in different directions. A small muscle at the bottom of each spine pulls the spine to make it stand up.

Arctic Hare

In the far north, the Arctic hare shares its snowy habitat with eagles, falcons, and wolves, so it has to be quick on its feet to stay out of trouble. The pads of the hare's feet are covered with thick fur in winter, giving extra grip and protection from the cold. Its coat changes color with the seasons to provide camouflage throughout the year.

Social Status

▶ The Arctic hare often lives alone, but it can also be found in groups of several hundred.

WHERE DO THEY LIVE?

The harsh environment of the North American tundra—a vast, flat, treeless, arctic region.

North America

Group Work

◀ The Arctic hare group works as a team when feeding. Some stand guard while the others eat. They also cluster together to share body warmth.

FACTS

SIZE

- It can grow up to 26 in (66 cm) from nose to rump.

- The Arctic hare is one of 21 species of hare found worldwide.

- It is bigger than a rabbit.

DID YOU KNOW?

- The ears are short. This means there is less body area to lose heat from in the subzero climate.

- The Arctic hare can survive low temperatures that many animals of a similar size could not.

- The front teeth never stop growing because they never stop being worn down.

Eyes and Teeth

▶ The hare's eyes are set high on each side of its head to give good all-round vision, even when it is feeding head-down. The front teeth have chiseled edges for nibbling at tough heather stems, tree shoots, and grasses.

Black Rhino

The black rhino has a huge head, a massive body, and thick, heavy limbs—but it is also surprisingly flexible and fast. These rhinos live alone, apart from a mother with young offspring. They mark out their territory with dung piles and urine.

WHERE DO THEY LIVE?

Pockets within sub-Saharan Africa.

Sahara Desert

Africa

Color

▶ Black rhinos are gray. The name comes from the color of local mud when dried onto the rhino's skin.

DID YOU KNOW?

The flexible upper lips hold on to vegetation when feeding.

The neck and shoulder bones have spiny parts to hold the muscles that support the huge head.

Rhinos have poor eyesight but excellent hearing—their cone-shaped, moveable ears can pinpoint sounds.

Infants

◀ At three days old, a young rhino can follow its mother around. The mother and calf stay together for the first two to three years, until the next calf is born.

FACTS

SIZE

● Black rhinos can charge at 31 mph (50 km/h).

● They feed mainly on leaves and branches from shrubs and trees.

● They live for up to 30–40 years.

Fearsome Horns

▶ The two horns are used mainly for defense and for display. They are made of keratin, the main ingredient in human hair and nails. Not only does the horn scare off attackers, but it is also a weapon that can toss a lion into the air.

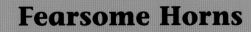

Plains Zebra

Also known as the Burchell's zebra, it lives on the plains of East and Southern Africa. It has a similar build to a horse, being 8ft 3 in (2.5 m) long—not including the bushy black tail. It is the most common type of zebra and the kind found most widely across Africa.

Social Groups

▶ Zebras are often seen in small groups of a male (stallion), several females (mares), and their young (foals).

WHERE DO THEY LIVE?

East and southern Africa.

Africa

Patterning

◀ Each zebra has a unique pattern on its body. This might be to allow herd members to recognize each other from some distance away.

FACTS

SIZE

- The plains zebra is smaller than the other two zebra species.

- The coat of a zebra is brown and white when it is born.

- Northern zebras have narrower striping.

DID YOU KNOW?

- Plains zebras can live alongside wildebeest. They call warnings to each other when predators approach.

- The stripes might be a kind of camouflage, making it hard for a predator to tell one from the group.

- Plains zebras are under threat from hunters.

Habitat and Food

▶ Plains zebras generally live in treeless grasslands. They can live at sea level or up on Mount Kenya at 14,100 ft (4,300 m). They travel 700 mi (1,127 km) each year to follow the rains. They mainly eat grass of different types. The plains zebra is in danger from lions and spotted hyenas, as well as Nile crocodiles when it is crossing rivers. Olive baboons attack foals, but not adult zebras.

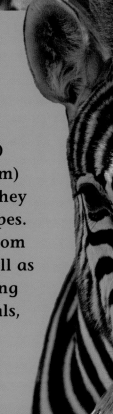

Japanese Macaque

Long, thick fur and a strong, compact body help the Japanese macaque to survive the cold winters of northern Japan. They live in forests, both deciduous—where the leaves fall off the trees in winter, and coniferous—where the trees are green all through the year.

WHERE DO THEY LIVE?

Japan

Found on three of the four main islands of Japan: Honshu, Shikoku, and Kyushu.

Appearance

▶ They have a brown fur that is lighter on the back and thighs. The face and rump are a reddish color.

Group Position

◀ There are three times as many females in a group as males. If a mother is powerful in a group, her infant will also be seen as a powerful member.

FACTS

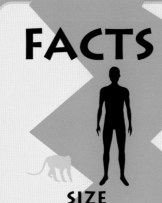

SIZE

● To keep warm in the cold winter they plunge into hot springs.

● They are not shy of humans.

● They live for up to 30 years.

DID YOU KNOW?

✋ Macaques live in groups known as troops around a core of related females.

✋ A monkey walks on the soles of the flats of its feet, rather than on its toes. This makes its walk look plodding.

✋ The monkeys' tails help with balance but have poor circulation, so they can suffer from frostbite.

Diet and Teeth

▶ The Japanese macaque is omnivorous but doesn't eat meat. It eats insects such as beetles and cicadae as well as plants, fruit, and soil. It has the same number of teeth as a human, but the canine teeth of the male are much longer.

Ring-tailed Lemur

The ring-tailed lemur is the best known of the lemur species. It has a long catlike tail with black and white rings. It is active during the day, mainly eating fruit and nuts. It lives for 16 to 19 years. Lemurs can communicate with their group using many different sounds.

WHERE DO THEY LIVE?

Like all lemurs, it only lives on Madagascar, mainly in the southern and southwestern parts.

Madagascar

Running Free

▶ Unlike most lemurs, which live mainly in trees, it spends a third of its time running on the ground.

DID YOU KNOW?

🖐 It lives in groups of males and females up to 20 in number. These are known as troops.

🖐 The long tail acts like a warning flag. It gives off a scent in fights between males.

🖐 They have specialized hands, with a sharp claw on each front foot for cleaning themselves.

Infants

◀ Infant lemurs weigh 2.5 oz (70 g) when first born. They are carried on the mother's chest for the first two weeks and after that on the mother's back.

FACTS

SIZE

● It lives in forests and dry scrub areas.

● Both sexes have a dark scent gland near each wrist.

● In the mornings it is often seen sunbathing to warm itself.

Pointed Features

▶ The pointed muzzle has a moist, doglike nose. The lemur uses its nose to smell how ripe fruits are, as well as for reading the scent markings of other lemurs. It has bright yellow or orange eyes that are surrounded by black "spectacles" of fur.

Tarsier

Small enough to fit in the palm of a human hand, this odd-looking primate has the huge eyes and swiveling head of an owl and springs about like a tree frog. It is a keen hunter and mainly comes out at night. It only eats meat. The tarsier gets its name from its long tarsal (ankle) bones, which help propel it while leaping.

WHERE DO THEY LIVE?

Asia

In Borneo, Sumatra, Sulawesi, and the Philippines in Southeast Asia.

Huge Eyes

▶ Tarsiers have enormous eyes and a head that can rotate almost a full circle.

Special Digits

◀ The long, slim fingers have lumps at their tips to help the tarsier keep its grip. The middle finger is as long as the upper arm.

FACTS

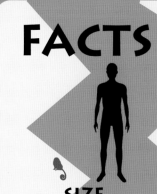

SIZE

- It mainly eats insects but also birds, lizards, and bats.

- Powerful jaws allow it to open its mouth very wide.

- It can live for up to 12 years.

DID YOU KNOW?

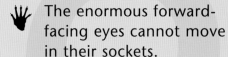 The enormous forward-facing eyes cannot move in their sockets.

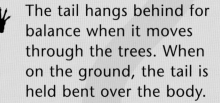 The tail hangs behind for balance when it moves through the trees. When on the ground, the tail is held bent over the body.

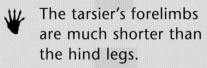 The tarsier's forelimbs are much shorter than the hind legs.

Paws and Fur

▶ Tarsiers use their paws to hold on to a vertical branch, where they will sleep during the day. They cling to branches and move about with leaps of up to 19 ft 7 in (6 m)—30 times their own body length. The soft fur changes in color from ivory-yellow in Sumatra to gray in the Philippines and golden-orange in Borneo.

African Elephant

The elephant uses its trunk for feeding, smelling, trumpeting, and hosing itself down. Herds are made up of females and their offspring, with males forming their own small groups. They are intelligent animals, showing signs of humor, memory, and sadness.

Herd Leader

▶ Elephants roam over large areas. They move in herds led by a senior female elephant who knows the territory well.

WHERE DO THEY LIVE?

Once widespread in Africa, mainly south of the Sahara Desert, now less evenly distributed.

Sahara Desert

Africa

The Young

◀ Herd members are extremely protective toward their young. Females will challenge predators such as lions that attack young elephants.

FACTS

SIZE

• The elephant is the world's largest land mammal.

• Tusks can grow up to 11 ft (3.3 m) long.

• Each ear can be 4 ft (1.2 m) across.

DID YOU KNOW?

● Elephants flap their ears backward and forward to cool down.

● The tusks used to be incisor teeth, but have developed. They are made of ivory and never stop growing.

● There is a fatty cushion on the bottom of the foot that can spread under the elephant's weight.

Elephant's Trunk

▶ The trunk is highly flexible. It is capable of both powerful and delicate movements. The nostrils at the tip are very sensitive. Controlled by 100,000 muscles, the trunk can pick up small objects.

American Beaver

The beaver's waterproof overcoat and strong teeth make it suitable for a life of labor in the water. It builds dome-shaped wooden lodges that have underwater entrances hidden from predators. It is the largest rodent in North America and the third largest in the world.

WHERE DO THEY LIVE?

Most of North America from the Arctic Circle across Alaska and Canada to northern Mexico.

North America

Sitting Up

▶ Beavers will often sit up on their hindquarters, especially when they are gnawing through saplings.

Insulation

◀ The coat is made up of two types of hair. Short, dense hair forms an insulating undercoat, while an overcoat of longer, coarser hair keeps the undercoat dry.

FACTS

SIZE

• It has a lifespan of up to 20 years.

• It eats leaves, ferns, grasses, algae, twigs, and woody stems.

• It can fell trees up to 19.75 in (50 cm) in diameter.

DID YOU KNOW?

• Two of the claws are split on the hindfoot. These act like combs for grooming.

• Each hindfoot is webbed between the toes. This gives the beaver paddle power underwater.

• The head is quite square, containing the sharp incisor teeth and powerful jaw muscles.

Incisor Teeth

▶ The beaver has two pairs of large incisor teeth that grow continuously. The front faces of the teeth are harder than the rear. When the faces rub together, they wear at an angle, giving a chisel edge.

American Red Squirrel

The American red squirrel is also known as the chickaree and pine squirrel. It lives mainly on pine cone seeds. Each one must have its own feeding territory separate from other squirrels before its first winter. Offspring fight for a territory or occupy a new one.

WHERE DO THEY LIVE?

They are found across Canada and in the USA east of the Rocky Mountains.

North America

Food

▶ They mainly eat seeds from plants, but can also eat mushrooms, tree leaves, berries, and birds' eggs.

Young

◀ Mothers give birth to litters of between three and four offspring each year. The offspring are pink and hairless and weigh about 0.33 oz (10 g).

FACTS

SIZE

- Less than a quarter survive their first year.

- They are active during the day.

- They carry mushrooms up onto tree branches to dry them.

DID YOU KNOW?

✋ Red squirrels are smaller than other North American squirrels.

✋ Mammals such as martens, coyotes, gray foxes, red foxes, wolves, and lynxes eat American red squirrels.

✋ Birds such as large owls, eagles, crows, and northern goshawks eat American red squirrels.

Mothers and Nests

▶ Before giving birth, the mother makes several nests out of grass and among tree branches. She will move her young between different nests in her territory. Sometimes a mother squirrel will give all or part of a territory to her young.

Black Rat

Scent is very important for the black rat, which mostly comes out at night. Its senses of sight and hearing are also well developed. Despite its name, the black rat is actually more often gray-brown above and pale gray, or even creamy white, beneath. Rats are very flexible—they can fit through a hole the size of a quarter.

WHERE DO THEY LIVE?

Alongside humans in many habitats across tropical and temperate regions of the world.

Worldwide

Whiskers

▶ Touch-sensitive whiskers along the snout of the black rat help it feel its way around in dim light.

Infants

◀ Female black rats produce three to six litters a year of up to ten young each time. The black rat lives for about two to three years.

FACTS

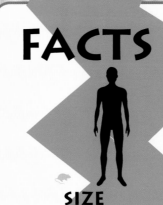

SIZE

● They are nocturnal.

● They are classified as a pest because they eat crops, spread disease, and damage buildings.

● They are mainly herbivorous.

DID YOU KNOW?

✋ The black rat lives in large packs of up to 60.

✋ It carries many diseases, including bubonic plague. This killed 25 million people in Europe in the fourteenth century.

✋ The hairless tail, longer than the head and body combined, provides balance when climbing.

Claws and Paws

▶ There are four long, clawed toes on each forepaw, and five on each hindpaw. The rat uses its toes to grip and run along ropes or power lines, and its claws to cling and climb on rough surfaces. Black rats are very nimble and are good swimmers.

Cape Porcupine

The porcupine's excellent senses of hearing and smell, plus its mass of thorny quills, allow it to detect and repel predators. It has a very effective defensive technique of lodging itself in a hole with only its spines exposed above ground.

WHERE DO THEY LIVE?

In much of Africa south of the equator in a wide variety of habitats.

Southern Africa

Warning Sign

▶ Hollow "rattle" quills are attached to the tail by a stem. These are used to sound a warning.

Infants

◀ Infant cape porcupines are born with their quills and spines. These are soft until they are exposed to the air, after which they become hard.

FACTS

SIZE

- Cape porcupines can charge backward.

- They are mainly herbivorous but eat some carrion.

- They have a lifespan of 20–30 years.

DID YOU KNOW?

 All feet have four toes. The hindfeet also have a tiny "thumb."

 The bulbous snout may help the porcupine sniff out buried bulbs and roots in dry ground.

 Cape porcupines live in complex burrows, where both parents care for the young in a "clan" system.

Defensive Quills

▶ The cape porcupine has defensive black and white quills and spines on its back. These grow up to 20 in (50 cm) and can be made erect when threatened. Barbed tips on the quills and spines hook into the flesh of predators, breaking away from the porcupine's body.

Harvest Mouse

The harvest mouse is most active around dusk, when it uses its rather large eyes in the weak light. They are most easily seen in the summer, when they sleep in nests above ground. During the winter they tunnel and keep a store of food in their burrows.

Seeking Food

▶ It searches for food using the stalks of plants as walkways, aided by its grasping tail.

WHERE DO THEY LIVE?

Western Europe extending into Asia from Russia, across to China and Korea.

Europe

Asia

Under Threat

◄ The harvest mouse is under threat from modern farming methods. They do not have enough places to build their nests, and they cannot find enough to eat.

FACTS

SIZE

● The harvest mouse weighs about the same as a medium-sized coin.

● The only European rodent that has a prehensile tail.

● One of the world's smallest rodents.

DID YOU KNOW?

❧ Its body is a maximum of 3 in (8 cm) long. The tail is roughly the same length.

❧ The last 0.75 in (2 cm) of the tail is prehensile. Strips of muscle across the underside allow the tail to grasp.

❧ Mothers carry their young in their mouths.

Toes and Eyes

► Each slim foot has a padded sole. The outermost of the five toes is set apart from the rest. This helps the mouse to grip while climbing. This toe also allows it to handle food and to groom itself. The mouse's eyes are close to the muzzle.

Aardvark

The name of this animal comes from the Afrikaans words meaning "earth pig," although the aardvark is not in fact related to pigs. It has a huge appetite and can eat up to 50,000 termites in a night. It rips the nest apart, probing inside with its long, sticky tongue and drawing the insects into its mouth.

Burrows

▶ Aardvarks use their claws to create underground burrows, digging tunnels up to 43 ft (13 m) long.

WHERE DO THEY LIVE?

Sahara Desert

Africa

Across much of Africa below the Sahara, but not in west-central parts of the Horn of Africa.

Tunnels

◀ Aardvarks sleep in the day and come out of their burrows in late afternoon or after sunset. If attacked in a tunnel, an aardvark will seal the tunnel off behind itself.

FACTS

SIZE

- It lives alone in a complex burrow system.

- It has a diet of termites and ants but also eats cucumbers.

- It has a lifespan of up to 10 years.

DID YOU KNOW?

 The aardvark does not have any close relatives living today.

 It has no canine or incisor teeth, but has continuously growing cheek teeth that grind up insects.

 It can burrow very quickly into hard soil to escape from predators.

Snout and Ears

▶ The trunklike snout has a disk-shaped, mobile nose that is used to sniff out prey. The dense hairs around the nostrils keep out soil and sand. The ears are tall and quite slender. They can detect the tiny scrabblings of termites. The ears can also be moved independently of each other to help detect possible predators, especially during feeding.

Giant Anteater

The giant anteater is built to track down insects. It breaks into their colonies and laps them up with its long, sticky tongue. Its main defense involves standing on its rear legs and slashing out with its front claws. It has a very powerful sense of smell, 40 times that of humans.

Solitary

▶ Giant anteaters are solitary, wandering creatures. They occupy large areas, staying in different nests.

WHERE DO THEY LIVE?

Southern Mexico to South America, east of the Andes, south to northwest Argentina.

South America

Long Snout

◀ The giant anteater has a long, thin snout that grows up to 18 in (45 cm). It also has a long, sticky tongue that can reach up to 24 in (60 cm) from the mouth.

FACTS

SIZE

- They can eat up to 30,000 termites a day.

- Their tongue can move in and out of a nest 160 times a minute.

- They have a lifespan of up to 26 years.

DID YOU KNOW?

 The sharp front claws can rip apart the wall of ant or termite nests.

 The bushy, fanlike tail provides shade during the day and acts as a thick blanket at night.

 When the tail is held over its body while resting, it acts as a camouflaging cloak.

Physical Traits

▶ The anteater has no teeth, and its eyes, brain, and mouth are tiny for an animal of its size. It can eat several thousand ants or termites in a few minutes. The tongue also has tiny backward-pointing spines to drag out the insects.

Glossary

Agile – moves quickly and easily

Aquatic – growing, living, or found in water

Binocular vision – sight using both eyes over the same field. An animal with binocular vision, such as humans, has a better idea of how far away objects are.

Bulbous – looking like a bulb; rounded

Burrow – a tunnel dug into the ground by an animal

Camouflage – hiding by disguising with colors and patterns

Canines – the sharp, tearing teeth of a meat-eater

Carnassial – the cutting teeth of a meat-eater

Carnivore – an animal that only eats meat

Carrion – the body of a dead animal that provides food for other animals

Conical – shaped like a cone

Domestic – connected to the home Cats and dogs are domestic pets, in contrast to wild animals such as coyotes

Endangered – the risk of no more of the species being alive

Forequarters – the part of the body that consists of the forelegs, shoulders, and joining parts

Gait – the pattern of footsteps at various speeds, such as the walk, trot, canter

Grizzled – having dark hairs mixed with gray or white

Hemisphere – either the northern or southern half of the Earth which is divided by the equator or the eastern or western half which is divided by a meridian

Herbivore – an animal that only eats plant-based food, such as grasses, fruits, and vegetables

Hibernation – a time when some animals become less active in order to conserve energy. They slow down the speed at which they breathe, lower their body temperature, and survive on stored fat.

Hindlimb – back leg

Hindquarters – the back legs and the part of the body above them

Larvae – a developing insect in its first stage after coming out of the egg; a grub or caterpillar

Membrane – a thin layer of tissue that covers or lines parts of the body

Migration – the traveling over long distances by animals looking for food sources when the seasons change

Muzzle – the part of an animal's face that sticks out – its nose and jaw

Nocturnal – active at night

Palate – the top of the inside of the mouth

Predator – the animal that is hunting

Prehensile – a part of the body, usually a tail, that has adapted to grasp and hold objects, such as branches

Prey – the animal that is hunted by a predator

Repel – to drive back

Sapling – a young tree

Savannah – a flat grassland in tropical or subtropical regions

Solitary – alone

Subspecies – a group of related organisms that can interbreed and are geographically distinct from others in their species

Tapering – narrowing

Warren – a network of underground interconnecting burrows

Index